GUIDELINES

adult
ministries

*Ministries that Help
Adults Love
God and Neighbor*

Richard H. Gentzler, Jr., Bill Lizor, and Debra Smith
General Board of Discipleship

ADULT MINISTRIES

Copyright © 2008 by Cokesbury

ISBN 978-0-687-64682-1

Some paragraph numbers for and language in the Book of Discipline *may have changed in the 2008 revision, which was published after these Guidelines were printed. We regret any inconvenience.*

Contents

Welcome

You are so important to the life of the Christian church! You have consented to join with other people of faith who, through the millennia, have sustained the church by extending God's love to others. You have been called and have committed your unique passions, gifts, and abilities to a position of leadership. This Guideline will help you understand the basic elements of that ministry within your own church and within The United Methodist Church.

Called to Spiritual Leadership

Each person is called to ministry by virtue of his or her baptism, and that ministry takes place in all aspects of daily life, in and outside the church. As a pastoral leader or leader among the laity, your ministry is not just a "job," but a spiritual endeavor. You *are* a spiritual leader now, and others will look to you for spiritual leadership. What does this mean?

First, *all* persons who follow Jesus are called to grow spiritually through the practice of various Christian habits (or "means of grace") such as prayer, Bible study, private and corporate worship, acts of service, Christian conferencing, and so on. Jesus taught his disciples practices of spiritual growth and leadership that you, as a disciple, are to share with others as they look to you to be a model and guide.

Second, it means that you always keep your eye on the main reasons for any ministry—to help others grow to a mature faith in God that moves them to action on behalf of others, especially "the least" (see Matthew 25:31-46). This is an aspect of "disciple making," which is the ultimate goal of all that we do in the church.

CULTIVATING VISION AND MISSION

As a spiritual leader, a primary function you carry is to help those you lead to see as clearly as possible what God is calling your church to be and to do. Ideally, your church council first forms this vision and then forms plans and goals for how to fulfill that vision. As a leader, you will help your team remain focused and accountable to honor the vision and goals to which the church is committed. You will help your team create and evaluate suggestions, plans, and activities against the measure: *Does this move us closer to our church's vision to bring others to God in this place and time?*

CHRISTIAN CONFERENCING

While there are appropriate and useful business-like practices that apply to church life, Christian practices distinguish the church as the church. In the United Methodist tradition, how we meet and work together is important. "Christian Conferencing" involves listening not only to each other, but also listening intently for the will of God in any given task or conversation. This makes prayer essential in the midst of "business as usual." As Christians, we are called to "speak the truth in love." This is a special way to speak in which we treat one another as if each of us were Christ among us. As a spiritual leader in your ministry area, you have the privilege and opportunity to teach and model these practices. By remembering that each of us is beloved of God and discerning the presence of God in all that the church does, every task becomes worshipful work.

THE MISSION OF THE UNITED METHODIST CHURCH

The United Methodist Church is a connectional church, which means in part that every local church is interrelated through the structure and organization of districts, conferences, jurisdictions, and central conferences in the larger "family" of the denomination. *The Book of Discipline of The United Methodist Church* describes, among other things, the ministry of all United Methodist Christians, the essence of servant ministry and leadership, how to organize and accomplish that ministry, and how our connectional structure works (see especially ¶¶125–138).

Our Church is more than a structure; it is a living organism. The *Discipline* describes our mission to proclaim the gospel and to welcome people into the body of Christ, to lead people to a commitment to God through Jesus Christ, to nurture them in Christian living by various means of grace, and to send persons into the world as agents of Jesus Christ (¶122). Thus, through you—and many other Christians—this very relational mission continues.

(For help in addition to this Guideline and the *Book of Discipline*, see "Resources" at the end of your Guideline, www.umc.org, and the other websites listed on the inside back cover.)

Biblical and Theological Foundations

i n the closing verses of Matthew, Jesus tells his followers to "go therefore and make disciples" (Matthew 28:19). The book of Acts succinctly describes the practices of the infant church as devotion to "the apostles' teaching and fellowship, to the breaking of bread and the prayers" (Acts 2:42). The apostle Paul reminds early church congregations of the necessity of "[equipping] the saints for the work of ministry" so that they would come to maturity, rather than being "tossed to and fro and blown about by every wind of doctrine" (Ephesians 4:11-14).

Called to Lead

You have been called to work with other leaders in the church to fulfill the church's mission to make disciples of Jesus Christ for the transformation of the world. As a leader of adult ministries you have a unique responsibility to provide leadership in your congregation so that adults in all of their life stages, from young adults to midlife adults to older adults are
- accepted as beloved children of God
- provided opportunities to relate to God through worship, prayer, and other spiritual disciplines
- nurtured in the faith through Bible study, mutual accountability, and other faith-forming practices
- sent out as disciples of Jesus Christ through which God will transform the world.

The *Book of Discipline* states that the function of the local church "is to help people to accept and confess Jesus Christ as Lord and Savior and to live their daily lives in light of their relationship with God" (¶202). As the body of Christ, we are challenged to take the gospel of Jesus Christ to all people.

YOU ARE NOT ALONE

Just as the members of the early church were empowered by the Holy Spirit to witness through their words and actions to God's love, the Holy Spirit will work through you and others. As you engage individually and with others in those practices described in the book of Acts—welcoming, worshiping, learning, and serving—you will experience God's grace and be empowered to lead other adults as they grow in faith.

The Task

the United Methodist Church recognizes young adulthood as beginning at approximately age eighteen. The life expectancy in the United States is around seventy-seven years. So most people can expect to spend at least sixty years in some phase of adulthood. During those years adults will have a wide variety of life experiences. Some will marry and some will not; some will have children and some will not; some will spend years gaining a formal education and some will not; some will have been part of a church family since birth and some will not. The list can go on and on. Planning for ministry with people who represent such a wide range of ages, needs, concerns, and interests can seem daunting. Depending upon their context, congregations have developed various organizational structures to be in effective ministry with adults in their church and community. Regardless of your church size or structure this Guideline is designed to help equip you in leading adult ministries in your congregation.

Responsibilities of the Adult Coordinator

Depending upon your congregational structure, your job title may be Coordinator of Adult Ministries, Coordinator of Young Adult Ministries, Coordinator of Middle Adult Ministries, Coordinator of Older Adult Ministries, Coordinator of Single Adult Ministries, Coordinator of Marriage Ministries, or some other title that indicates you have a particular leadership role related to adult ministry. The coordinator's role is not necessarily to do all the ministry work but to keep the big picture in view and to work with others, if possible, on a comprehensive strategy that is appropriate for your congregation's context. Within those broad boundaries, you are responsible for:

- becoming familiar with the overall goals of your congregation and how these goals are achieved through the congregation's ministry with adults
- encouraging and extending the goals of the congregation through adult ministry
- identifying and articulating the needs of adults in the local church
- helping to plan and carry out a varied and wide-ranging ministry with adults, including worship, study, fellowship, and service opportunities
- being a liaison with organizations, people, and resources that relate to adults and their concerns for personal growth and service
- bringing Christian vocation as a calling to ministry in all spheres of life before the congregation
- supporting and guiding the work of the adult council (or other organizational structures specific to your congregation) throughout the year, planning agendas, and presiding at meetings
- becoming aware of resources and programs for adults

- keeping the congregation informed about the hopes and concerns of adults of all ages and life situations in your community, the goals of adult programs, and the resources available that will help your congregation reach these goals
- reviewing and evaluating programs as they affect the Christian faith formation of adults
- representing concerns of adult ministries at the church council and charge conference
- taking part in and being accountable to the charge conference through the church council.

TRAINING FOR YOUR JOB

From time to time, the church offers workshops and seminars that can help you in your ministry. Such training events may be a district or conference workshop or other training seminar in your area. Check with your pastor, the committee on lay leadership, your district superintendent, and conference council staff to find opportunities that match your training needs.

You can consult these people or agencies for help:
- your pastor
- adults in your congregation and community
- adult coordinators in other congregations
- your church council
- your district adult ministries council or district adult ministries coordinator
- your conference council staff, conference adult coordinator, or conference adult ministries council
- General Board of Discipleship Staff (see Resources for more information).

The Roles of the Adult Coordinator

Whether you are the coordinator of all adult ministries or a specific segment of adult ministries (young adult, older adult, and so forth), you fulfill a crucial role of leadership in the life of the congregation. Since adults make up the majority of members in most congregations, the work of the coordinator heavily influences the life of the church. Your position as leader can involve several roles.

If you are the coordinator, then you will want to take seriously the various roles you will be expected to assume. If you are a member of the adult council, education committee, or nurture committee, you will want to be aware of the roles the coordinator is expected to fulfill and how you can assist in carrying out this important job.

SERVANT LEADER. First and foremost you are a leader, a servant leader. You were chosen because you have exhibited the qualities needed for such an important position in your congregation.

As a leader in the church you are expected to be growing in the Christian faith. A servant leader is open to God's will and seeks to be faithful and obedient to God. Helping adults become disciples of Jesus Christ is an important role for the coordinator of adult ministries. This role requires such skills as the ability to listen to the needs of others, compassion, discernment, and scriptural understanding. As a leader of adults, you are on a spiritual journey and have the privilege and opportunity to invite others to join in the pilgrimage.

A leader has people skills, administrative skills, and planning skills. You will need to attend to relationships and to the personal contributions and well-being of each member of the group, balancing the concern for accomplishing a task with tending to the feelings and concerns of group members.

A leader in the church understands and supports the mission of the church. Become informed about church policies and procedures. Accept and help clarify the vision of the church that guides the planning of the church council. Two expressions of commitment to the church's mission are active participation in all aspects of the church's life and financial support of its mission.

You set the pace for the work of the adult council (or committee or task force or team) by carefully planning the agenda, keeping members informed, involving members in decision-making, and seeking at all times to embody what it means to be a Christian disciple.

VISIONARY. An important role for the coordinator will be "to dream dreams" and "see visions." Helping to envision what is possible and what is needed can be a crucial role to play. You will be called upon to "think big," but at the same time not to lose touch with the limitations of the situation. A vital part of our United Methodist theology is the desire "to go on to perfection." Thus, we are challenged to strive for the best—for God's vision—of how and where we ought to be God's people.

EVALUATOR. A key to good leadership is the ability to evaluate what is happening in the present. Seek to understand and properly evaluate present programs. Are they working? Are they meeting needs? Are they focused on missions? Are they helping people grow in faith? Are they helping to fulfill the church's ministry of reaching out and receiving people, enabling them to relate their lives to God, equipping them for ministry, and sending them back into the world as faithful disciples?

PLANNER. The adult council is charged with planning ministries that will involve adults in learning, sharing, and serving. You will work with the adult council to evaluate present programs, define the role of the council in the context of the church's mission, plan for meaningful programs, enlist leaders, and implement whatever is planned. The ability to lead the council in planning may be one of the most important roles the coordinator will fulfill.

ADVOCATE. The coordinator will serve as an advocate for adults in the various groups that plan and administer the church's ministry. You will report to the church council on the mission and goals of the adult council and advocate for those adults who are left out or whose needs are being overlooked in church programming. Advocacy may take many forms, all the way from seeking more financial support for adult ministries and planning retreats for single parents to providing caring outreach to older adults in long-term care facilities.

IDENTIFYING AND INVITING LEADERS. You will want to strive constantly to identify potential leaders for various aspects of adult ministry. In addition, you need to be involved in inviting them for specific responsibilities of leadership. Who in your congregation would be good teachers? Who would be good leaders for task forces set up to carry out specific projects? Who has gifts and talents that could be used in working with older adults? Who would be able to provide leadership for a singles ministry program? Who could work with and help young adults grow in their faith?

If you have questions about your role, consult with your pastor or chair of the church council. In addition to this Guideline, consult the *Book of Discipline* and other resources available through your church office or library.

Getting Started

how might a local church develop an intentional ministry among adults? The following ten steps will help you and your congregation design a ministry with, by, and for adults.

1. ORGANIZE A COUNCIL

If there is no adult council, find one other person who shares your vision for adult ministry in your church. Begin looking for others who are especially interested in sharing your vision. Review the names of people with your pastor and committee on nominations and leadership development and consider the suggestions they make. Organize an adult council (or committee or task force or team) of six to fifteen members depending upon the age demographics and membership size of your local church. In order to have a cross section of all adults, the council should include women and men; people who are single, married, divorced, and widowed; people representing a variety of ages and stages; persons with disabilities; and persons representing multiracial and multicultural diversity. After the adult council is approved by the charge conference, the council may be administratively related to the church council, committee on education, or other related committee.

While some churches may just have one adult council, others will have several councils (teams, task forces, committees) organized around specific life stages or experiences. For example, a church might have a young adult council or an older adult council.

2. GATHER INFORMATION ABOUT ADULTS

Develop a survey instrument for gathering information about the adults in your local church and community. Invite and train members of the adult council to visit in the homes of adults. If more people are needed for completing the survey, invite and train other church members to help with the personal interviews. It is important to identify your audience by collecting as much information as possible, such as:

- name, address, phone number, and other information-type questions
- information about their needs as adults
- information about ways they, as adults, can be in service to others.

For large membership churches, you may wish to develop "focus groups" instead of door-to-door surveys. Focus groups represent a sampling or cross section of all adults in the church and community. Ask specific questions concerning needs and interests of adults in the focus group setting.

3. IDENTIFY EXISTING CHURCH PROGRAMS

Review church programs and activities for the previous year or two. Identify all the programs and activities that involved adults. Remember that the church should provide the ministries that only the church can; this is what separates the church from being a community organization. Evaluate the effectiveness of the program and determine whether the activity is an ongoing event.

As you review church ministries, consider what is provided for people who are seeking meaning in their lives and are just beginning to consider the church. These sorts of ministries need to be nonthreatening and need to introduce people to the Christian faith. Also consider what ministries are available for people who are new to the church. Just because people are over the age of eighteen does not mean that they are well versed in Bible, Christian heritage, or other elements of the faith.

Look at what is offered for those who are more mature in their faith. Faith maturity does not necessarily correlate with age. A young adult may have a very mature faith and an older adult may be a new Christian. As people mature in their faith, they need opportunities to probe more deeply into Scriptures—reflecting on everyday life in light of the Bible's teaching, deepening their prayer lives, and reaching out to others with the love of Christ.

4. IDENTIFY EXISTING COMMUNITY PROGRAMS

Identify community programs, organizations, and activities that involve adults from your local church. Take a survey of their programs and services. If a community organization is providing a program that is successful, don't try to compete, but do explore whether a partnership is desirable and feasible. Identify ways adults can be involved in community service.

5. DESIGN A PROGRAM OF MINISTRY

After you have interviewed the adults in your church (and community when feasible), evaluated existing church programs, and identified community organizations and programs, you are ready to develop programs by, with, and for adults in your church and community. If your adult council discovers several programs that need to be developed and implemented, select the programs or activities your church will be able to do and prioritize the list.

6. IDENTIFY RESOURCES AND KEY PERSONS

Secure the necessary financial and material resources needed to reach your goal. Invite and train selected persons to serve as key resource personnel.

7. IDENTIFY OTHER CHURCHES AND AGENCIES

Working with other churches and agencies is often an excellent way to get a program started. By combining forces with others, you may actually save time, money, and resources.

8. SET GOALS AND OBJECTIVES

Goals will identify what program you want to have, who will lead, who will participate, and when it is to be done. Objectives will identify how you plan to accomplish your goals.

9. IMPLEMENT THE PROGRAM

After establishing a timeline for implementing the program and the various process steps along the way, put the plan for ministry into action.

10. EVALUATE

Your goals and objectives should be evaluated periodically to determine the effectiveness of the program. If feedback warrants it, continue the program. If it does not, begin the process over again.

Stages of Adult Development

growing up" is a lifelong process. In order to work effectively with adults in ministry, you need to know something about the adult life cycle and the kinds of needs, interests, and concerns adults experience at various stages of adulthood.

It is clear that adults go through many changes in a normal life span of seventy to eighty years or more. We generally think of at least three stages of adulthood: young, middle, and older (see "Adult Developmental Characteristics," pages 24-25). These categories are not very precise or helpful unless we explore in more depth the kinds of needs, issues, and concerns faced during these broad periods of adulthood.

Development implies change. The change may be good or bad. You can help adults of all ages grow toward spiritual maturity by providing a caring and challenging environment for study, reflection, and action. As a leader in adult ministry, you will want to help develop a comprehensive ministry that will enable people to grow in faith and faithfulness as Christian disciples.

Development is also cumulative. Adults who participate actively in the full range of worship, learning, and service opportunities through the church will grow in their faith and discipleship as they grow older. Remember that adults bring with them the values of their generation. World events, demographics, technological advances, and societal norms are just a few of the influences that will shape a generation in a particular manner. (See Generational Snapshots on pages 19-23).

Young Adulthood

The essence of the young adult experience can be expressed in one word—*transition*. No longer a youth, but not yet "grown-up" enough to feel like an adult; young adults find themselves in the midst of a life of choices, decisions, and pressures. It is during this life-stage that important discoveries about one's identity, purpose, and inner makeup are often made. Physiologically, as individuals move into adulthood their brains begin to move into post-formal thinking. Suddenly, multiple truths are an option and multiple paths toward "the truth" are often accepted and explored.

Young adulthood is also often characterized by a feeling of being alone—a separation from familiar world of family and friends. Home often takes on new meaning as young adults find themselves going off to college and/or work in places far away from where they grew up. Thus, another transition occurs, and young adults are forced to learn how to cope with life and survive on their own. It is during this time when relationships, especially core friendships, become central to a young adult's development.

The five most common transitions experienced during the young adult years are: graduation from high school, graduation from college, entrance into the work world, marriage, and having children. Obviously, not every young adult experiences all five (or even more than one) of these transitions, but these are generally attributed to young adulthood. These physical transitions, as well as the mental development discussed previously, work together to stretch and grow young adults as they move toward full adulthood.

The young adult experience is a time of rich and rapid social and psychological development in addition to physical change in body and the world in which they live. Thus, the challenge becomes finding one's place in this new world and assuming responsibility for one's life as a developed adult. It is this process—the journey toward one's identity and place in the world—that prepares the young adult for the next transition to middle adulthood.

Josh and Heather are twenty-six years old. They have been dating for two years and are seriously contemplating marriage. Neither has ever been connected to a church. They recently started attending a Sunday school class for young adults at your church. They have decided that they want to be more involved in the life of the church. What opportunities will you provide for Josh and Heather to assist them in their growth as disciples and in their desire to enter into a marriage relationship?

Middle Adulthood

The core years of middle adulthood are approximately ages forty to sixty, but the boundaries are very porous. Some people experience the transition from young adulthood to midlife in their early thirties while others are still dealing with what are traditionally considered young adult issues into their forties. At the other end of the continuum some, particularly those who experience early retirement, may consider themselves older adults in their mid-fifties while others may define themselves as being in midlife until well into their seventies. Most physical abilities peak in young adulthood and begin to decline modestly as people move into middle adulthood. The need for reading glasses or bifocals is often the first sign of this.

Because of the wide variety of life situations that are the norm for people at midlife, the issues they face are diverse. Many have been married at least once, but a significant number have divorced and may or may not have remarried. They may be the parents of young children, adolescents, and/or young adults. Many are also grandparents. During midlife most people will experience the death of at least one parent and/or begin to deal with the realities of aging parents.

At midlife people begin to shift from thinking about how long they have lived to how long they have left to live. This often results in a midlife review as they consider what they want to accomplish in the rest of their lives. Making meaning of life is a major developmental task as people begin to ask, "So what difference does it make that I've been on this earth for forty or fifty years?"

John and Linda are forty-seven years old. Both work in demanding jobs. Their parents are in their eighties and are beginning to face declining health. Their teenage son is going through some difficult times, and their daughter, graduating from college and unable to find a job, is moving back home. They attend worship services but are not involved in other learning and service activities in the church. They say they are too busy to take on any major church obligations. What kind of study, fellowship, or service opportunities might appeal to John and Linda that would nurture their faith?

Older Adulthood

Older adulthood can be a time of creative growth and development, or it can become a time of stagnation and despair. Older adulthood is described less by chronological years and more by attitude, function, and lifestyle.

Older adulthood can be described as two phases: early older adulthood and late older adulthood. In early older adulthood, adults may be adjusting to reduced income, retirement, changes in their health or the health of their spouse, death of their spouse, and establishing a new social network to replace their work network. In late older adulthood, adults may experience limited mobility, loss of autonomy, need for assistance and care, loneliness with loss of family and friends, and a sense of finitude and mortality.

At this stage of life, adults are dealing with issues such as finding worth in one's being, not through having or doing; claiming one's life journey and faith story; confronting losses and acknowledging gains; defining areas of dealing with independence and dependence; experiencing a new (or renewed) relationship with God through Jesus Christ; and serving the needs of others.

Some of the faith needs of adults at this stage of life include the need to know that God loves them, to experience a church that cares about older adults as individuals and as a group, to serve as mentors and role-models for the benefit of succeeding generations, and to have available support systems for coping with losses.

Catherine is eighty-three years old. Last year her husband of sixty-two years died. Since then, she has struggled with adjusting to life alone. She is in reasonably good health, but she has withdrawn from many of the church and social activities she formerly enjoyed. She is having difficulty deciding about her living arrangements; and though she has a car, she really should not be driving. She has no family members living nearby. What can you do through the older adult ministry of your congregation to make sure Catherine is nurtured and able to maintain her independence and, at the same time, is challenged to keep on growing and serving?

Common Life Experiences of Adults

It can be helpful to look at adult stages of development in the categories described in the previous pages. However, there are threads of common experiences faced by adults of all ages. You will want to keep these common experiences in mind as you plan your adult ministry program.

RELATIONSHIPS

A basic need of all human beings is to be related to other people in meaningful ways. When these relationships are strained or broken, adults face the need for support and healing. Among the most painful experiences are death, divorce, and serious illness. Contrary to our stereotypes, death or serious illness can occur at any age. Even divorce occurs across the spectrum from young to older adults. In these times of crisis, the church can play an important role in caring, supporting, and healing.

The loss of a job is an experience that has become commonplace for young and middle adults. Many experts believe that the idea of having the same job for more than five years is a thing of the past. Losing one's job can be a very stressful time for an individual or family. How can your adult council help people cope when changes in the workplace threaten the economic well-being of your members?

Other changes in relationships (somewhat more age related) may include the birth of a child or grandchild; children starting school, going away to college, or getting married; changing jobs, having to retrain for a different job and establishing new collegial networks; or moving to a new home and community and having to establish new friendships.

PERSONAL CHANGES

Adults of all ages may experience physical, psychological, or spiritual changes that can cause great anxiety. Physical or mental illness can strike at any age and bring about drastic changes in personal and family life patterns. Heart disease, Alzheimer's disease, cancer, and other health problems change thousands of lives each day. Experiences of spiritual awakening, or even loss of faith, can also occur at any time. You will want to be sensitive to the wide range of personal changes going on in the lives of adults in your congregation. Think of ways of ministering to them as they work through these difficult times.

Generational Snapshot: The Millennials

Born between approximately 1982 and 1999, the members of the millennial generation began to enter young adulthood in 2000, and in 2008 over 70% of young adults were part of the millennial generation. By 2012 virtually all young adults will be from this generation.

- Also known as Generation Next or Generation Y.

- The most diverse generation in the United States.

- The first generation to grow up in a world where technology such as computers, cell phones, and television have always been a driving force within the overall culture.

- This generation often blurs the line between "parent" and "friend" with their Boomer elders. This has led to parents becoming much more active in the lives of their young adult children. In extreme forms this is referred to as "helicopter parents" (hovering over their young ones).

- Relationships, be they family, friends, or colleagues, are at the center of this generation's lifestyle.

- Being one of the first generations to grow up in a completely "customizable" world, Millenials are often criticized as feeling entitled, expecting things to be given to them exactly as they want.

- View faith as a communal process and find fulfillment through identity within faith communities. Unlike previous generations, these young people are likely to participate in several faith communities (not necessarily from the same denomination or even the same religion).

- Workplace satisfaction is greatly related to high recognition and praise from supervisors and colleagues.

- Driven to action for causes that they feel are worthwhile. Unlike the individualistic Postmoderns, Millenials' social action is most often seen as a communal event.

- The bombing of the Oklahoma City Federal Building, school shootings like Columbine High School, and the 9/11 attacks have all played a huge role in the development of this generation's social identity.

(Based on "Generational Snapshots: Postmoderns & Millennial." © 2007 General Board of Discipleship)

Generational Snapshot: Postmoderns

Born between about 1965 and 1981, many in this generation either have or soon will be transitioning from young adulthood to middle adulthood.

- Often referred to as Generation X, the 13th Generation, or the Echo Boom Generation.

- Due to stress and isolation caused by transitions from home and the "quarter-life crisis," Postmoderns often view themselves as alone. Thus, there is a sense of individualism and a lack of a cohesive generational identity.

- An often forgotten generation because they are wedged between the Boomers and the Millennial (the two largest generations in the adult age-span).

- Often thought of as a "slacker" generation, Postmoderns express a more laid-back approach to the world than their Boomer predecessors. Much of this attitude comes from Postmoderns' experience of a world with a high divorce rate, over-dedication to "work," and the rise and fall of the dot.com era.

- Seeing corporate and moral decay in the culture around them, many Postmoderns have developed distrust for authority (and in many cases, by extension, institutions as a whole).

- Distrust for authority often spills into the workplace. Often seen as the cynics, rebels, and young "boat rockers" tired of "business as usual," who aim to change what they view as stagnant corporate policies.

- Seek to experience life and work for themselves rather than being guided or prescribed a particular path to the answers.

- While mission and service rank high in the Postmodern value system, they are seen as individual events. The Postmodern is likely to say, "If the world is going to change, I have to be the one to do it."

- View faith as an experience tied to the individual. Community is expressed in terms of a small group as opposed to an identity within an overall faith community.

- The explosion of the space shuttle Challenger is the major formational event for this generation. While it had a huge impact on the generation, it caused no real movement in the generation's social principles or the fiber of the culture.

(Based on "Generational Snapshots: Postmoderns & Millennial." © 2007 General Board of Discipleship)

Generational Snapshot: Baby Boomers

Born between approximately 1946 and 1964, this large generation represents most of the people currently in middle adulthood. The first of this generation will reach 65 in 2011.

Health
• Cancer is the leading cause of death
• About two-thirds are overweight
• Lower back pain is the most common health issue followed by high blood pressure.

Life Events
• 88% have been married at least once
• 40% have divorced
• 29% have remarried
• 36% have lost a job
• 49% have a father who has died
• 30% have a mother who has died
• 35% have become grandparents

Employment
• Comprise 43% of the workforce
• 87% of men are working
• 75% of women are working
• In about 70% of Boomer couples, both spouses are employed

Households
• About 60% include married couples
• Average household is 2.5 people
• More than 60% of younger Boomers and a third of older Boomers have children under age 18.
• Among older Boomer women nearly 18% live alone.

Spending
• Are the nations biggest spenders
• Have rapidly increasing health care costs
• Are the nations biggest debtors

Attitudes
• Are more similar to younger adults than older adults in their assessment of their personal lives.
• Consider family and friends the most important and satisfying aspects of their lives, with their religious and spiritual lives next.
• Report less satisfaction with their personal finances and their work lives than any other aspects.
• Female Baby Boomers are more likely to report a high degree of satisfaction with their spiritual lives than are male Boomers.
• Race and ethnicity play a larger role in shaping Baby Boomer attitudes toward life than do age, gender, income, or education.

Frequent Issues
• Aging parents
• Work and pre-retirement
• Death of a parent
• Parenting school-aged children
• Adult children returning home
• Finding balance in their lives
• Coming to terms with unfulfilled dreams and expectations, or fulfilled dreams that have failed to live up to expectations.

(Based on: "A Quick Look at Baby Boomers," InFormation Adult Ministries. Winter 2006. © General Board of Discipleship. Used by permission.)

Generational Snapshot: Older Adults

The older-adult population—people 65 years or older—numbers 36.8 million. The projected older adult population is expected to increase to 71.5 million by 2030.

Population

- About one in every eight, or 12.4%, of the population is an older adult.
- The 85+ population is projected to increase from 4.2 million in 2000 to 6.1 million 2010 (a 40% increase) and then to 7.3 million in 2020 (a 44% increase for that decade).
- There are an estimated 80,000 centenarians (people 100 years or older) in the United States.
- Older women outnumber older men at 21.4 million older women to 15.4 million older men.
- There are 72 men for every 100 women in this age group.
- Members of ethnic minority groups are projected to increase from 5.7 million in 2000 (16.4% of the elderly population) to 8.1 million in 2010 (20.1%) and then to 12.9 million in 2020 (23.6%).

Life Expectancy

- Women reaching the age of 65 can expect to live another 19.8 years (nearly 85).
- Men reaching the age of 65 can expect to live another 16.8 years (nearly 82).

Education

- 72% have at least a high school diploma.
- 18% have earned a bachelor's degree or higher.

Living Arrangements

- Of householders 80% are home owners and 20% are renters.
- About 31% (10.7 million) of non-institutionalized older adults live alone (7.9 million women and 2.8 million men).
- While a relatively small number (1.56 million) and percentage (4.5%) live in nursing homes, the percentage increases dramatically with age, ranging from 1.1% for people 65–74 years to 4.7% for people 75–84 years and 18.2% for people older than 85.
- Half of older women age 75 and older live alone.
- Approximately 5% of the elderly live in self-described senior housing of various types (including assisted living); many have supportive services available to their residents.

Jobs

- More than 5.3 million are in the labor force.
- By 2014, 8.7 million will be in the labor force.
- Comprise 11% of the nation's business owners

Health

- Nearly 74% assessed their health as excellent, very good, or good.
- 26% indicated that their health was fair or poor.

Generational Snapshot: Older Adults

Income (from the 2000 census)
- Median income is roughly $21,102 for men and $12,080 for women.
- Median family income of home-owners is about $25,353.
- Median family income of renters is about $13,540.
- 42% of older householders spend more than one-fourth of their income on housing costs—35% for home owners and 76% for renters.
- The poverty rate is about 10.1%.
- Major income sources: Social Security (90%), income from assets (56%), private pensions (30%), government pensions (14%), and earnings (23%).

Voting
- 79% were registered to vote in the 2004 presidential election.
- 71% of citizens in this age group reported actually casting a ballot in the 2004 election.

Elder Care
- More than 10 million elderly, or nearly one-third of the older adult population, need some type of long-term care.
- Many older adults do not have the financial resources and lack private long-term care insurance, and thus must rely on help from family caregivers.

Family
- 54% are married and living with a spouse.
- 30% are widowed.
- Older men are more likely to be married than older women—72% of men versus 42% of women.
- 43% of women are widows.
- About 671,000 grandparents aged 65 or over maintain households in which grandchildren are present.
- Over 415,000 grandparents aged 65 and over have primary responsibility for grandchildren living with them.

Geographic Distribution
- About half (52%) live in nine states: California, Florida, New York, Texas, Ohio, Pennsylvania, Illinois, Michigan, and New Jersey.
- Constitute at least 14% of the total population in 8 states: Florida, West Virginia, Pennsylvania, North Dakota, Iowa, Maine, South Dakota, and Rhode Island.
- Most (77.4%) live in metropolitan areas. About 50% in suburbs, 27.2% in central cities, and 22.6% in non-metropolitan areas.

(Based on U.S. Census Bureau data and The Graying of the Church *by Richard H. Gentzler, Jr. Discipleship Resources)*

Adult Developmental Characteristics

	Young Adults	Midlife Adults	Older Adults
Physical	Measure time since birth; learning preferences and abilities are established by age 20; reach physical peak	Begin to measure time as "time till death"; coming to terms with mortality; midlife physical changes	Learning ability may be affected by hearing and sight losses; increasing health care needs and chronic illnesses
Psycho/Socal	Developmental task: *Intimacy vs. Isolation* (Erik Erikson)—needing others vs. being emotionally distant; finding place in society and in community; struggle with independence, identity, and intimacy; early stages of occupation and relationship building	Developmental task: *Generativity vs Stagnation* (Erik Erikson)—serving others vs. being self absorbed; range of interests include career planning, personal growth, relationship development, problem solving, and values clarification	Developmental task: *Integrity vs. Despair* (Erik Erikson)—life has meaning vs. a life of regrets; adjustment to retirement; loss of relationships due to death; increasing dependence upon others; volunteerism and care-giving are important
Emotional	Entering adult world; intimacy; settling down; need to be accepted	Managing midlife transitions such as death of parents, children leaving home, parenting, and aging parents	Need to be valued, respected, and accepted by people and institutions
Intellectual	Learn best when not under stress; time is valuable; prefer problem-centered learning over subject-centered; want to apply learning to daily living	Self-directed learning; want to be involved in decisions about learning; want input from knowledgeable people, resources, and groups	Build on life experiences; use visual images and mental pictures to enhance learning; encourage self-paced and problem-centered learning activities

Adult Developmental Characteristics

	Young Adults	Midlife Adults	Older Adults
Spiritual	Many seek spiritual experiences; may be returning to church; some want answers; others want chance to raise questions and search	Want to understand the meaning of life and one's place in the world; focus on values and priorities; take responsibility for one' own spiritual journey	Want arena to grow in faith and make sense of life story; need purpose and to feel life is worth living; may want to share one's life and faith story and to mentor others
Special Needs	Want to be treated and respected as adults and peers; want arenas for fellowship, service, and ministry to others	Learning context is important; climate for learning and thinking; traumatic events or life transitions often prompt involvement in learning activities	Opportunities for continued growth; significant service vs. busy work; daytime activities and accessible surroundings; good lighting and acoustics
Gifts to Share	Expanding knowledge, creativity, and intimacy; willingness to take risks	Dependability; steadiness; concern for the future; financial resources	Wisdom; time; endurance; objectivity; life experiences; hope; acceptance of death
Vocation	Seeking fulfilling work; on the job training	Questioning; reaping; career changes; mentoring	Retirement from primary career; may re-enter or reinvent work
Expectations of the Church	Often want answers or a safe place to search	Want help in making meaning of life and finding balance	Stability; place for friendships; sacramental nature of church

(From *InFormation: Adult Ministries* by Richard H. Gentzler. © 2004 General Board of Discipleship. Used by permission.)

Tools for Your Work

On the following pages you will find a variety of worksheets, forms, and articles that will assist you as you plan and carry out adult ministries. While some of the items can be used directly as provided, most will provide you with a starting point that you can adapt based on your particular context.

Consider Your Context

As you think about what it means to be in ministry with adults in your church and community, reflect on these questions. Your responses will help you think about the people of your community (including your congregation) and how your congregation's ministry with adults might serve them best. You may want to discuss these questions with others in your congregation and community.

• What three concerns and what three hopes do you believe adults have about their community and their faith? How do these relate to living as Christian disciples and good neighbors?

• What three experiences might help adults understand more about how the Bible and the Christian faith can be resources for daily living?

• How could the overall quality of life be improved for at least one specific group of adults in your community?

• What existing or new programs should your congregation sponsor for these adults?

My vision or hope for our congregation's adult ministries:

_____

_____

I will take the following steps toward making my vision a reality:

_____

_____

Assessing Your Adult Ministry

Your role as "evaluator" is an important one. You will need regularly to ask, "How well are we doing?" This section is designed to assist you in assessing your present ministry with adults. You may wish to use the suggestions here or develop your own approach to evaluating your present ministry with adults.

As adult coordinator, assist your congregation in living out its primary task of reaching out and receiving all people into the faith community; helping them relate their lives to God through Jesus Christ; nurturing them in the Christian faith; and equipping, sending, and supporting them as faithful disciples.

REACHING THOSE NOT YET A PART OF THE CHURCH FAMILY

An essential aspect of our ministry involves reaching out and receiving people just as they are. How well are you doing in reaching those who have been "outsiders" and those members who are only marginally involved?

Adult members and constituents	Number
All adults (those over age 18)	
Young adults (approximately 18–30)	
Midlife adults (approximately 31–64)	
Older adults (approximately 65 and above)	
Married adults	
Single adults	

Current Involvement in adult ministries	Number
Sunday School	
Bible Study	
Covenant Groups	
United Methodist Men or Women	
Other (list)	

Who isn't involved in the adult ministries of the congregation?	Involved	Not Involved
Young married couples		
Divorced people		
Adults with disabilities		
People who work on Sunday		
Homebound adults		
Other (list)		

REACHING YOUNG ADULTS

List current ministries in place that relate to young adults. Check the boxes to indicate what groups of young adults participate in this ministry.	Single	Married	College Students	Those Choosing Paths Other Than College	Working Professionals	Young Parents	Other (list)

What are some additional programs or activities that might be needed to minister more adequately to and with your young adult constituents?''

In what settings other than church facilities can ministry opportunities be offered?

How is time of day and day of week factored in to planning strategies?

What might you need to do to make ministries not specifically targeted for younger adults more welcoming and nurturing to people in this age group?

REACHING MIDLIFE ADULTS

List current ministries in place that relate to midlife adults. Check the boxes to indicate what groups of midlife adults participate in this ministry	Single, Never Married	Divorced	Widowed	Married	Grandparents	Parents With Teens	Other (list)

What are some additional programs and activities that might be needed to enhance your ministry with middle adults?

What opportunities are you providing for people at midlife to reflect upon their life experiences from a faith perspective?

How is your church in ministry with members who are going through difficult life transitions such as dealing with aging parents, going through divorce, loosing a job, and so forth?

REACHING OLDER ADULTS

List current ministries in place that relate to older adults. Check the boxes to indicate what groups of older adults participate in this ministry.	Healthy-Active Adults	Home-bound Adults	Living in Retirement Communities	Married	Single	Living in Long-term Care Facilities	Other (list)

What are some other programs and activities that might be needed to enhance and provide a more comprehensive ministry by, with, and for older adults?

In what settings other than church facilities can ministry opportunities be offered?

How is time of day and day of week factored into planning strategies?

A Comprehensive Plan: Settings

It is important that adults be given choices in the types of programs and ministry opportunities offered in and through their local congregation. An intentional and comprehensive system for forming adult disciples will include the following elements.

STUDY

Study settings within the program of Christian education are an essential ministry of the local church and should be high in your priorities for adult ministry. Christian education and formation settings may include Sunday school classes and groups, weekday Bible study (such as DISCIPLE), short-term classes on specific topics of current interest, workshops, leader training, and various small groups. Learning is central to discipleship formation and growth. To be a disciple is to be a "learner." Therefore, any adequate program for adults will include a variety of opportunities for adults to learn and grow.

SPIRITUAL GROWTH

Spiritual growth groups and opportunities are at the heart of the church's ministry. Small groups established for short- or long-term spiritual development may find resources such as *Companions in Christ* helpful. Events such as the Walk to Emmaus lead to other opportunities for Christian spiritual support and growth.

NURTURE AND FELLOWSHIP

Fellowship settings are equally important for a well-rounded program in adult ministry. Many adults come to church primarily for fellowship. The church offers a special kind of fellowship that cannot be found in just any group or organization. As the "body of Christ," we are concerned about one another so that when "one member suffers, all suffer together," and when "one member is honored, all rejoice together" (1 Corinthians 12:26). Adults need to feel cared for, and they need to care for others. This dual need can be partly met by fellowship groups and activities in the church.

Fellowship opportunities may be especially significant for single adults of all ages, adults who live alone, families with young children, and older adults who may be cut off from other family members and former work colleagues.

Adult Sunday school classes and other small groups are often excellent settings for fellowship, not only on Sunday mornings, but also through a variety of other activities and events. Many adult classes have regular fellowship suppers and other social affairs that meet at other times besides Sunday mornings.

SUPPORT AND ACCOUNTABILITY

Support and accountability settings provide growth opportunities in safe, nurturing environments where adults encourage, support, and hold one another accountable around challenges of daily living and Christian discipleship. Spiritually inspired leaders and supportive parishioners move adult fellowship to deeper, more meaningful ministry levels in settings where adults discuss life experiences and reflect from a faith perspective on relationships, health issues, career and professional choices, vocational transitions, and life-stage transitions.

These gatherings can be significant times for personal fueling and refueling. Activities may range from informal discussion groups to structured methodical gatherings with specialized instruction or instructors. Covenant Discipleship Groups are one example of structured accountability groups that focus on Christian discipleship. Regularly scheduled gatherings, consistent attendance, and active participation are crucial.

MISSION AND SERVICE

Mission and service opportunities are a critical component of sending adults back into the community and world to live as disciples of Christ. Some avenues of service may include outreach ministries such as Habitat for Humanity, Meals on Wheels, feeding the hungry, visiting the homebound and those in nursing home or long-term care facilities, tutoring children and youth, and a variety of outreach ministries that may be particular to your own congregation and community.

Mission and service opportunities may need to be coordinated with your mission/outreach council or chair. This coordination is usually achieved in the church council.

LEADER DEVELOPMENT

Leader development is essential to an effectively functioning system of adult ministry. Those who are asked to assume responsibilities in the church need to be provided training and orientation for their jobs. Sometimes this function is assigned to a "leader development" council or committee. No matter how training programs are planned and administered, they need to be an intentional component of the adult ministry plan. Equipping people for leadership in the church and for leadership in the community is an essential part of adult ministry.

The leaflet *A Comprehensive Plan for Teacher Development in United Methodist Congregations* (see Resources on p. 40) provides guidance for developing a leader development plan.

LOOK AT YOUR CURRENT SETTINGS

Use this chart to help you identify current settings for adults in your congregation. Empty boxes on the chart may indicate opportunities for new ministry settings.

	Young Adults	Midlife Adults	Older Adults
Study			
Spiritual Growth			
Nurture/ Fellowship			
Support/ Accountability			
Mission/ Service			
Leadership Development			

A Comprehensive Plan: Components

Developing a comprehensive ministry plan will help ensure that you have processes in place to reach out to all people, relate their lives to God through Jesus Christ, help them to grow in Christian faith, and send them back into the community to do God's work in the world. Use the checklists on pages 35–37 with your adult council or other groups to help develop a ministry plan that will include the following components.

REACHING AND RECEIVING

Are you reaching out and receiving all people? Our concern for adults must express itself in our evangelistic mission of witnessing to our faith and inviting others to become a part of our faith fellowship. All people are the object of God's love and concern. We do not make a distinction in our reaching out; however, we do identify and address distinctive needs (for example, divorce adjustment, widowhood, nursing home living).

EQUIPPING FOR DISCIPLESHIP

How are you equipping people for their Christian discipleship? The author of Ephesians tells us that the Holy Spirit has provided all of us with gifts to "equip the saints for the work of ministry, for building up the body of Christ, until all of us come to the unity of the faith and of the knowledge of the Son of God, to maturity, to the measure of the full stature of Christ" (Ephesians 4:12-13).

"New" Christians need special attention. You will have adults coming into your church who have little experience of "church" and who have practically no background in Bible study or Christian education. (Do not assume, though, that lifelong members consider themselves well-advanced in their own faith formation.) They, and lifelong members of the congregation, need to continue to grow and mature in faith over the whole course of their life-time.

SENDING FORTH

Are you sending forth people to be Christian disciples in the world? The strength of the church is not measured in terms of the numbers of people who come to the church but by what happens in the world as a result of their having come. It is easy for a church to become ingrown, to be focused on what is going on inside the church building. The ultimate test of effective discipleship in and through a congregation or an individual Christian is to be found in the family, the workplace, the political arena, and in relationships with neighbors. Through Christian disciples, God is transforming the world.

Reaching and Receiving

Use this checklist as a springboard for discussion to help your adult council consider how you are currently reaching and receiving adults and what you need to add or change.

Which of the following describe your congregation?

____ Good signage that directs people to adult classes, small groups, worship, and so forth.

____ A regularly updated website that provides basic information that someone considering your church would want to know (mission, vision, and core values, classes, small groups, expectations of members, worship times, calendar of events, how to find the church, and so forth.)

____ Greeters who intentionally introduce visitors to others in the congregation with whom they can easily relate.

____ A system of visitor welcome and follow-up that is hospitable.

____ Intentional opportunities for adults of all ages who are curious about the Christian faith to encounter and engage with members of your congregation in a positive and nonthreatening manner. This might include activities that occur off site such as church softball teams, groups that use church space such as AA or other recovery groups, community events sponsored by the congregation, outreach ministries that serve the community, and so forth.

____ Trained mentors and guides who walk with newcomers as they enter the life of the congregation.

____ A spiritual gifts assessment process to help everyone in the congregation including newcomers discover and use their spiritual gifts.

____ A comprehensive communications system that ensures members and visitors are kept up-to-date on congregational news. This may include newsletters, telephone chains, websites, e-mail lists, announcements, and so forth.

____ An intercessory prayer ministry that supports adults at all life stages.

____ Long-time members constantly monitor themselves to ensure they are not being inhospitable by using acronyms and other language that exclude others, assuming that "everybody already knows...," and adopting attitudes of "this is the way we have always done it" or "we tried that once before."

Equipping for Discipleship

Use the following scale to evaluate each statement related to participation in your congregation. Use the results to help determine how you are currently equipping adults for discipleship and what needs to be added or changed.

NA: Opportunities are not available   **F: A few people**
M: Most people   **E: Nearly everyone**

___ Participate in classes or small groups that introduce people to the Bible.

___ Participate in classes or small groups that study the Bible in depth.

___ Understand our Christian heritage.

___ Understand the unique contributions of The United Methodist Church.

___ Participate in a class or small group for support and accountability such as a Covenant Discipleship Group.

___ Participate in corporate worship.

___ Participate in leading worship (choir, liturgist, usher, and so forth).

___ Participate in a prayer ministry.

___ Regularly share how God is at work in their lives.

___ Fast as a spiritual discipline.

___ Tithe.

___ Participate in intentional reflection about how their faith influences their everyday lives.

___ Have a plan for personal spiritual growth.

___ Teachers and small group leaders regularly participate in training and other learning opportunities that strengthen their abilities as spiritual leaders.

___ Have regular opportunities to be in relationship with people of different ages, cultural backgrounds, and economic conditions.

___ Participate regularly in the sacraments of baptism and Holy Communion.

___ Listen to other's faith stories.

___ Tell their own faith stories.

Sending Forth

Disciples are formed so that the world might be transformed. How is the world—and specifically your community— more just, more compassionate, and more hopeful because God is working through the disciples in your congregation?

Which of the following describe your congregation?

__ Our congregation is known for its ministries of justice.

__ Our congregation is known for its ministries of compassion.

__ Our congregation is known for its ministry beyond our community.

__ Individuals in our congregation take leadership in community justice issues.

__ Individuals in our congregation are actively involved in making our community a safer and healthier place for the most vulnerable.

__ Our congregation regularly recognizes congregational members who are involved in ministry beyond our congregation.

__ Our congregation helps and encourages people to find places of service outside of the church building.

__ People from our congregation regularly visit those who are in jail or prison.

__ Our congregation has a system for identifying community needs and then addressing those needs.

__ Members of our congregation look for opportunities to share their faith with others.

__ Our congregation cooperates with other faith groups and secular groups to effect change in our community.

__ Our congregation spends more of its financial resources on outward focused ministry than it does on inward focused ministry.

__ Our congregation regularly organizes ministry opportunities that allow people with a wide range of skills and abilities to use their gifts to make a positive difference in the world.

Starting New Classes and Groups

This section will provide some practical steps for starting new study classes and other types of groups for adults. Program settings for adults include at least the following: study, spiritual growth, fellowship, leader training, and mission or service ministries.

WHEN IS A NEW GROUP NEEDED?

How will you know when you need to start new study classes and groups? If you answer yes to any of the following questions, then the time may be ripe for you to start a new group.

_____ Do you have less than 50 percent of your adult members attending Sunday school or other educational groups?

_____ Do you have at least six to eight people who might be interested in looking at a particular topic or issue?

_____ Do you have several people in the same age group who are not presently attending any type of study class or group?

_____ Do you have recent members who have not been incorporated into existing classes or groups?

_____ Do you have several people who are not able to attend current small group offerings because the meeting time conflicts with work or other obligations?

_____ Do you have several people currently going through a similar life transition (divorce, death of a spouse, birth of a child, job loss, and so forth)?

STEPS TO TAKE

Consider these suggestions as you start a new class or group.

1. Identify the potential group members.

2. Survey the potential members to determine areas of interest, concerns, or issues that may help identify class needs.

3. Make tentative plans for the type of class or group needed so you will have something concrete to offer.

4. Find someone who is willing to start the new group and will give leadership for a few weeks or months.

5. Write a letter to those who might be interested, giving them basic information about the proposed class. Invite potential members to respond to choices concerning the meeting time, day, and place.

6. Follow with personal contacts inviting prospective members to a meeting to discuss the new class. You may want this to be simply an informal discussion, or you may determine that the first meeting needs to be an organizational meeting.

7. If there is sufficient interest to start (at least six to eight persons), then set a date, arrange for a place to meet, and designate a leader(s).

8. Publicize the new class or group. Be sure to announce when the class will start, where it will be held, and something about its purpose. By publicizing the new class or group, you might spark the interest of some individuals who are still "sitting on the fence," or you might attract people you have previously overlooked.

9. Provide ongoing support during the early stages of the life of the group. The pastor, Christian educator or program director, and you can make certain that the group has the support of the church staff and the adult council.

A Final Word

Your job as coordinator of adult ministries is indeed an important one; it can make a difference in many lives. If you start to feel overwhelmed, remember that when God calls us to a challenging task, God also offers us the strength and guidance to perform the task. Remember also that you are part of a connectional church; there are people you can contact and a variety of resources to support you in a vital adult ministry.

Resources

**Indicates our top picks

THE GENERAL BOARD OF DISCIPLESHIP

Toll-free phone (877) 899-2780. (Note specific extensions.) Fax (615) 340-7071. Web: www.gbod.org
- Center on Aging & Older Adult Ministries, Richard H. Gentzler, Jr., director. Ext. 7173; e-mail: rgentzler@gbod.org
- Office of Young Adult and Single Adult Ministries, Bill Lizor, director. Ext. 7005; e-mail: blizor@gbod.org
- Office of Middle Adult Ministries, Deb Smith, director. Ext. 7135; e-mail: dsmith@gbod.org
- Office of Family and Marriage Ministries, MaryJane Pierce-Norton, director. Ext. 7170; e-mail: mnorton@gbod.org

GENERAL CHURCH PRINT RESOURCES
- *The Book of Discipline of The United Methodist Church–2008* (The United Methodist Publishing House, available from Cokesbury).

- *The Book of Resolutions of The United Methodist Church–2008* (The United Methodist Publishing House, available from Cokesbury).

BIBLE STUDY/CHRISTIAN EDUCATION WITH ADULTS
- *Beginnings.* A video and book small group study introducing the basic fundamentals of Christian faith, Christian living, and Christian community. Three studies available. Order through Cokesbury (800-672-1789)

- *A Comprehensive Plan for Teacher Development for United Methodist Congregations,* by the Christian Education Staff of the General Board of Discipleship. This 8-page leaflet is available for free download at www.gbod.org.

- *DISCIPLE: Becoming Disciples Through Bible Study.* Additional studies build on this one. A 34-week Bible study. For information write to: Disciple Bible Study, P.O. Box 801, Nashville, TN 37202-0801, or phone (800) 672-1789.

- *FaithLink.* A weekly resource helping adults connect faith and life as United Methodists. This resource is delivered weekly by fax or e-mail. To subscribe call (800) 672-1789.

- *Living the Good Life Together: A Study of Christian Character in Community.* Video and book small group curriculum series that includes study and practice of Christian character in daily life. Available through Cokesbury.

**• *Start Here: Teaching and Learning with Adults,* by Barbara Bruce (Nashville: Discipleship Resources, 2000. ISBN 978-0-88177-303-3). Designed for teachers of adults, this resource will help create learning environments where adults can grow in faith.

- *What's in the Bible and Why Should I Care?* A Bible study series guiding adults to find biblical insights into major life questions. Can be used in a variety of settings with several print and electronic editions. Order through Cokesbury (800-672-1789)

**• Look for more teaching and teacher helps at www.gbod.org/education and at SundaySchool: it's for life at www.sundayschool.cokesbury.com.

MIDDLE ADULT MINISTRIES
**• *Forty Sixty: A Study for Midlife Adults Who Want to Make a Difference,* by Richard H. Gentzler, Jr. and Craig Kennet Miller (Nashville: Discipleship Resources, 2003. ISBN 978-0-88177-325-5). A practical resource for leaders and middle aged adults who want to wrestle with issues and concerns facing this important stage in life.

- *Information: Adult Ministries.* A newsletter for leaders of adult ministries. Published by the General Board of Discipleship.

OLDER ADULT MINISTRIES
- *Adult Bible Studies*---a quarterly Bible study resource for adults, using the Uniform Lesson Series for weekly study and reflection. Available in print and compact disc formats for students and leaders. Order through Cokesbury (800-672-1789).

**• *Aging and Ministry in the 21st Century: An Inquiry Approach,* by Richard H. Gentzler, Jr. (Nashville: Discipleship Resources, 2008. ISBN 978-0-88177-540-2).

- *Building a Ministry for Homebound and Nursing Home Residents,* by Marie White Webb (Nashville: Discipleship Resources, 2003. ISBN 978-0-88177-403-0). Guide for developing ministry with homebound and nursing home residents.

• *Center Sage.* A newsletter for leaders of older adult ministries. Published by the Center on Aging & Older Adult Ministries, PO Box 340003, Nashville, TN 37203-0003. (877) 899-2780 ext. 7177.

• *Designing an Older Adult Ministry,* by Richard H. Gentzler, Jr. (Nashville: Discipleship Resources, 1999. ISBN 978-0-88177-269-02. For equipping local congregations in developing and maintaining intentional older adult ministries.

• *The Graying of the Church: A Leader's Guide for Older Adult Ministry in The United Methodist Church,* by Richard H. Gentzler, Jr. (Nashville: Discipleship Resources, 2004. ISBN 978-0-88177-409-2). This book examines who older adults are in our society and in our congregations, ways of motivating older adults in ministry, and helpful resources for leaders of older adult ministry.

**• *Living Fully, Dying Well Planning Kit,* by Bishop Reuben P. Job (Nashville: Abingdon Press, 2006. ISBN 978-0-687-33585-5). An excellent resource designed to assist adults in making careful, wise, and prayerful preparation for meeting life's most important moments. Resource contains Leader's Guide, Participant's Workbook, and DVD.

• *Mature Years.* Published quarterly, this resource is written specifically with older adult concerns in mind. Available from Cokesbury, (800) 672-1789.

• *New Beginnings: The Gifts of Aging* (DVD), by Richard H. Gentzler, Jr. (Nashville: Discipleship Resources, 2005. ISBN 978-0-88177-482-5). A 20-minute video resource for congregation and small group study showing creative ministries involving older adults in various settings including mission opportunities, intergenerational sharing, and service.

• *Remembering Your Story: Creating Your Own Spiritual Autobiography,* by Richard L. Morgan (Nashville: Upper Room Books, 2002. ISBN 978-0-8358-0963-4). With both a Leader's Guide and a Participant's Workbook, this resource for individuals and small groups is a valuable tool for helping people create their own spiritual autobiography.

• *Rock of Ages: A Worship and Songbook for Retirement Living* (Nashville: Discipleship Resources, 2002. ISBN 978-0-88177-373-6). *Rock of Ages* is a large print worship resource and songbook suitable for use with homebound and long-term care residents.

SINGLE ADULT MINISTRIES

• *InFormation: Single Adult Ministries.* A newsletter for leaders of single adult ministries. Published by the General Board of Discipleship.

YOUNG ADULT MINISTRIES

**• *Restless Hearts* Planning Kit (Nashville: Abingdon Press, 2008. ISBN 978-0-687-33566-4). A six-week study for reflection on God's care and presence in the midst of vocational journey.

• *Information: Young Adult Ministry.* A newsletter for leaders of young adult ministries. Published by the General Board of Discipleship.

• *Soul Tending: Life-Forming Practices for Older Youth and Young Adults,* by various authors with foreword by Kenda Creasy Dean and Ron Foster (Nashville: Abingdon Press, 2002. ISBN 978-0-687-03079-8). An effective resource that offers ways to engage the practices of the Christian faith- prayer, Bible study, worship, and spiritual friendship in everyday life; young people and adults are encouraged to lead as "co-journers" on the path to abundant life.

• *20/30: Bible Study for Young Adults.* A series designed for adult learners in their 20s and 30s. Each volume connects common everyday life themes to Scripture and group action. Available from Cokesbury, (800) 672-1789.

NOTES

NOTES

NOTES

NOTES

NOTES